Subtraction Isn't Always Less

Subtraction Isn't Always Less

ANN HUDSON

NEXT PAGE

Published by
Next Page Press
San Antonio, Texas
www.nextpage-press.com
© 2024 Ann Hudson. All rights reserved.

No part of this book may be used or reproduced in any manner without written permission from the publisher, except in context of reviews.

ISBN: 978-1-7366721-6-7
Library of Congress Control Number: 2024943851

BOOK TEAM:
Laura Van Prooyen, *director and editor*
Joni Wallace, *editorial consultant*
Amber Morena, *book designer*

Cover image: *Straße am Abend* (1913) by August Macke (translates to "Street at Night")

Contents

Wind Farms   -1-
Someone to Watch Over Me   -2-
The Lessons   -4-
Chaos   -5-
Order   -6-
Amphipods   -7-
Hawk Again   -9-
Brain Trust   -10-
June 19   -11-
I Still Address You Even Though I'm Talking To Myself   -12-
Rust   -13-
Second Grade   -14-
The Folk Songs of North America   -15-
Time and Temperature   -16-
The Way Men Leave   -17-
How to Get There   -18-
Green   -20-
Potential Energy   -21-
Azalea, Dogwood, Maple, Boxwood   -23-
Transit of Venus   -24-
Janus   -26-
Arrhythmia   -27-
Deathwish   -28-
Well   -29-
Syncopation   -30-

Bloom   -31-
Ways to Travel   -32-
Hippocampus   -34-
Catch   -35-
My Father Used to Read Books   -36-
Jellyfish   -37-
My Father's Knees   -38-
Blue   -39-
The Pond   -40-
Signals and Feedback   -41-
Afterlife   -42-
Blue Again   -43-
Red Geraniums   -44-
Torso of a Male Athlete (The Oil Pourer)   -45-
My Father's Hair   -46-
Last Day   -47-
Afterward   -48-
The Undertakers   -49-
Aftermath   -51-

Notes   -53-
Acknowledgments   -55-

Subtraction Isn't Always Less

Wind Farms

Their blades hum
    in the enormous
air. What became

    of the titanium hip
my father strode
    the world with?

Metal implants
    are melted down
and refashioned into

    almost anything —
why not this turbine
    I'm driving past, its

one eye pinned to me
    as it works and
works the empty spaces.

Someone to Watch Over Me

What better way to spend an hour
on this last day of May
than in the white tunnel
of the Magnetom, manufactured
in München, Germany in 2012
by Siemens. I stare at the sticker
and play with all the letters—
semen, mess, mine, immense, sin—
while the sonic wash machine thrums
and hammers around me. Kelly,
my tech, checks on me every so often,
and tells me I'm doing great.
To keep me company, she's
handed me headphones.
The music is tinny but amiable:
acoustic piano covers of standards.
I can pick out *Love is Here to Stay*,
Pennies From Heaven, and *Someone
to Watch Over Me*. My father is dead.
What's left of him is a box of ash
in a wall in a cemetery behind my
mother's house. He does not peer
over the edge of a cloud to check in
on his family and friends, responding
to the chime of our weeping, our fond
remembrances on his birthday,
our visits to the stone etched
with his name. He does not watch
over me as I am dipped into
this hammering river of magnets
and sound, this whirring, pulsing tube

that is imaging the inside of my body:
my bones, my tissue, the stones
of my remembering, the stones
of my forgetting, which I balance
one by one by one as carefully as I can.

The Lessons

Also why didn't you teach me
about the table saw in the shed?

And varnish? How am I supposed
to know about mitering, how

to caulk, or how long cement cures?
Before the internet there was you

and what you didn't know wasn't
worth knowing. Once school let out

you started planning our car trip
to the Midwest, studying the Rand McNally

until you memorized the route.
Each time you gassed up the car

you squeegeed the windshield,
careful not to drip, then popped

the glovebox to record the mileage,
the number of gallons, and the date.

Where are those tidy columns now?
Why didn't you teach me how

to drive a stick shift, how not to slip
backwards when I'm stopped on a hill?

Chaos

The flock of snowflakes
spirals, unfurling like a bolt
of lace that anyone
can walk through. Once
you could have taught me
how that system functions, its
regularity, its randomness.
And now the snow
just works. It always has.

Order

Trust me, I don't want to write
one more goddamn line
about my father. He lived,
he died. He's bone-rubble
in a hole in a cemetery wall.
He's in a cherry box the size
of the one the checks came in,
which, when the bank
returned them each month,
he slid back in the box
in consecutive order again.
Each box was dated and put
inside the cabinet, the cabinet
closed, the cabinet latched.

Amphipods

Bring me your tarot readings,
your psychic energies, your
reiki and shiatsu. I'm done
with the science I understand.
In every way today my brain
has failed me: too reasonable,
too rational, making the logical
choice. And where has it
gotten me? Time to stir up
some trouble, some babble,
some nonsense and chaos.
Look — even there a word
for something I know
from my father's articles:
how something that seems
random makes a pattern
we may be too close, too
far away, or at the wrong angle
to recognize. Bring me your
spirit guides, your angels,
your bedevilment. Bring me
things in languages no one
can recognize. Let me practice
listening with everything
except my brain. There are
creatures that can feed on bits
of wood that filter down
through the frigid waters.
Who wouldn't want to be
a creature that sustains
itself on shipwrecks? Kudos
to whoever sank down beyond

the limits of sunlight, well past
the point a human body
would be crushed by pressure
of the ocean, found gelatinous,
translucent strangeness there
and recognized it as life.

Hawk Again

It's a hawk in that oak again,
    another hawk or the same one
or not a hawk at all. It changes

    nothing if it is, except our desire line,
that electric bridge in the brain.
    Hawk, from a root which means

to seize, to grasp. What that hawk is
    and what it means are never the same.
We think our thinking reaches

    to the outer edge of consciousness,
but that's just the edge of our
    own awareness we're up against.

We're as stuck as that bird
    in a tree full of winter. And then
there's nothing there at all.

Brain Trust

After the hospital, there were trips to a doctor
every few days: neurologist, neurosurgeon, neural

psychologist, a daisy-chain of specialists. Awkwardly
we eased my teetering father into the passenger seat,

his scalp bristling with thirty staples, my hand hovering
over his white hair so he wouldn't scrape against the doorframe.

Mom sat tightly in the back while I fumbled with the mirrors.
In the waiting rooms, my father handed me

a yellow legal pad, and I filled pages as my parents answered
the questions they were able to. The neurologist ordered

an MRI though he warned us there may be blood deep in the brain
which could obscure a good image. My father's blood pressure

was a bit high but his heart was steady. Eighty percent
of the general population will have a fainting spell

in their lifetime; why my father fell in the night
is anyone's guess. A sleep event? The neurologist

expected he'd soon be able to walk to work again,
sit at his desk, but find it's hard to think. The notes stop here.

I've been reading them by the icy mailbox, sleet
ticking the yellow pages my mother sent in a sturdy envelope.

They turned up in his desk, her card explains.
They are your *notes*, she writes, as if I wouldn't recognize

the motion of my own hand, or maybe she means
here they are now, in my hand, fluttering a tiny bit. What's left.

June 19

Happy birthday, you bowl of dust,
you handful of ash, you you-not-you,
you figment of memory, you piece
of my own chronicle I continue
to address. You clicked off
like a beautiful, rattling light switch,
your cornflower eyes open.
I didn't want you to be scared. I wasn't
as I called out over my weeping sister,
my keening mother, *You're a good man*,
as if to let you know your work
is done, you're free to leave, as if
I had anything to do with it.

I Still Address You Even Though I'm Talking To Myself

I'm glad you died
when you did.
The way the porch
is part of the house
and part of the dark.

Rust

I still don't understand how rust
behaves, though I spent years

watching it bloom along the flank
of my father's Plymouth Valiant

whose engine transpositions
I can still hum along to.

Those brittle vinyl seats
chafed our thighs. Winter trees

blurred outside the window.
We peered through a stamp-sized hole

in the floorboards at the street
whirring past, the cold swirling

around our ankles. Dad
whistled in place of the radio.

Second Grade

By the time I'd rambled home
from the bus stop, my bookbag slung
on my back, the ambulance had come and gone
and someone had returned the ladder
to the garage and someone had driven
to the hospital and someone had even
raked away from the azaleas
the black fistfuls of leaves which
my father had clutched on his freefall
from the gutter, letting go only
once the ambulance arrived, his face
shiny with the pain of it, and it was only
the shadow of the ladder slicing
the golden curtain of sun on the kitchen wall
that made my mother look up
then step out to see what it could be.

The Folk Songs of North America

Awake in bed I listened to my father
tune up the guitar, the big, black songbook
opened to any one of his dozens

of favorite songs—*Shortenin' Bread*,
Hard Travellin', *Wabash Cannon Ball*.
I listened hard for *Big Rock Candy Mountains*,

held my breath so I didn't even rustle
the sheets, pondering *the buzzing of the bees
in the cigarette trees*, wondering how hens would lay

soft-boiled eggs, imagine splashing around
the lake of stew and whiskey, too. Who
could dream up such a baffling heaven?

Our family was too sensible even for white bread.
Every day in the cafeteria I unlatched
my lunchbox slowly, knowing I'd find

a crumbly, brown sandwich, an apple,
a thermos of milk, and two dry cookies I'd try
to nibble just the chocolate out of and not

be late for math, where Mrs. Wagner
would pace the aisles and try to convince me
that all squares are rectangles but not all rectangles

are squares, that fractions get smaller
as their denominators get bigger,
and that subtraction isn't always less.

Time and Temperature

How many times did I step into the den
to see my mother curled on the sofa,
her legs tucked to one side, one arm

crooked behind her head, the other hand
holding the phone to her ear as she listened,
eyes half-closed, to the announcement

of the local time and temperature? She kept
the number on an index card beneath the phone,
and when she called she heard no prediction

of the weather, no judgment of how
she'd spent her day, no demands
for dinner, no critique of her posture

or her sturdy hips, no muted shouting
behind a latched door, just infallible data,
re-orienting and precise. *The time is 6:49.*

Temperature 81. If I listened I could hear
the tick of her watch as she examined it.
I could hear her pull the tiny pin.

The Way Men Leave

They stand, adjust
their pantlegs, and walk
off with a nod. *Janette,*

my father'd say, *get
your purse.* She'd murmur,
and touch the wrist

of the woman she
was nearest to, she'd rinse
her glass twice and set it

in the sink, make her way
around the room to thank
the host and hostess.

My father stood on his heels
in the foyer, hands
in his trouser pockets,

fiddling with coins.
He'd drive them home,
headlights sweeping

the pitchdark trees. She held
her purse snapped shut
and upright on her lap.

How to Get There

We usually stopped at a Holiday Inn right off
the interstate, after roaring all day
through mountain passes and coal towns,

past tractor trailers whining down the incline,
past rest stops where we'd sometimes spread
a blanket in the grass so Dad could ease his eyes

and doze, where I'd race to the display rack
for a map of the whole state, determined
to trace our drive across each one

but never managing more than the next
few towns. I could only ask for so many Dixie cups
of lemonade before Mom would cut me off,

those sips by late afternoon warm and sweet-sour
because the mix would have settled
to the bottom of the gallon cooler.

After a day of driving with the windows
rolled down, of sitting on beach towels
over the vinyl bench seats, we would at last

pull in to a hotel, one with a pool he'd take us to
while Mom lay down. There'd be a restaurant
where we were allowed dessert, and then, worn out

from the drive and the queasy mix of warm
lemonade and maps, we'd turn in early.
Mom would tuck us in, click off the lamp,

then take her book into the bathroom to read.
I missed her. I wanted her back with us
in the dark, soft room, the AC rattling away,

the hiss of traffic from the interstate, the *thunk*
of the ice machine around the corner.
Dad was asleep in an instant, and soon

my sisters drifted off. The stiff, marigold curtains
were pulled tight across the windows so
the hotel room was lit only by the stripe of light

beneath the bathroom door, and I knew that no
matter what I wouldn't be able to sleep with that
bar of radiance. And then it was day.

Green

It was someone's idea to go out to the course
and hit a few rounds of golf. No one
but my father knew how to play.
We stood in an awkward bunch
and listened to his lesson: stand like this,
hold the club like this, do this with your elbows
and your knees. He moved all parts of himself
in smooth, synchronized arcs. I smiled like I
was having fun. My sisters each
took a swing, then I tried to do everything
he'd showed me, but my elbows locked,
my knees buckled. The golf ball
skittered off into grasses I could name:
switchgrass, dropseed, Little Bluestem.

Potential Energy

Curled scroll-like between the door handle
and the jamb is a pink leaflet the Jehovah's Witnesses

have left me. *Can the dead really live again?*
Would you say . . . yes? no? maybe? which at least exhausts

the possibilities. Apparently God hates death
and views it as an enemy. I trot to the bookcase

for a Bible to check the citations and out falls
the baseball card I've been looking for for years:

Ryne Sandberg, Cubs' second baseman
and my childhood crush. Baseball, beloved

by my father, bored me, the afternoons
yawning away in front of our black-and-white TV

with the crooked antennae, all the windows
thrown open but no air stirring, and baseball's

maddening pace deadening the hours. Still
Ryno's quick smile made a couple of innings

worth it. I slouched on the floor, too hot
to sit up, too hot to think. Dad leaned in

to the pitches, grumbled at the umps, scolded me
for turning the volume dial with my toes. Every love

is full of errors and resistance. Whatever insights
the Bible sheds on my dead father or baseball

or being lethargic and fourteen, whatever certainties
this pink pamphlet might promise, nothing's

as compelling as a moment of perfect suspension:
a ball midway between the mound and home,

full of energy from the pitcher's arm, headed for
the swing of the bat. Not *yes*. Not *no*. But *maybe*.

Azalea, Dogwood, Maple, Boxwood

A week home from the hospital,
my father stands, stooped and grinning
in his front yard, an eight-inch-long scab

across his scalp. My son crouches
with a jumbo yellow bat, waiting
for my father's pitch. I've made

some bad choices in my time but this one
takes the cake: letting my father
stagger past me to play baseball.

His hands are bruised from the IVs,
his eyes underscored with dark arcs.
I try to tell him he has little strength

and lousy balance, and my boy doesn't
understand how to be cautious.
But they've headed out and both so glad,

the screen door slamming behind them.
The best I can do is stand out by first,
mute and furious. My father lurches, tosses

a slow pitch which my son line-drives
to left field then runs the bases: azalea, dogwood,
maple, boxwood, throwing his arms

up in delight, while Dad staggers
to the ivy to hunt for the ball,
the glossy leaves shirring against his ankles.

Transit of Venus

My mother knows how any ordinary person
might be maimed by hot grease, the expressway,
or a pedicure, and somewhere in this teetering

pile of newspapers, birthday cards, and slips
of paper she's got the clippings to prove it.
She can recount a story about how boilers can

and do explode, then take you to the basement
to see where it happened. But memories are fickle,
and without the object—the picture leaning

against the library books on indefinite loan,
the postcard mailed from Rome so many years ago
all the writing has faded, the name and address

of an old friend long since moved away—
she wouldn't have that soft nudge
of remembering. Post-Its halo her place

at the table. My father, her husband of a half-century,
is reading the same three sections of *The Washington Post*
he's always read. There's no way to know

how much he can understand, or what his eyes
even focus on, but his hands remember how
to hold the grey page. There is a barbed row

of staples on his head; he doesn't remember
the fall, or calling each of his three children
from the hospital bed to say he was alive.

What he doesn't remember is still lodged
in his brain somewhere, as are the blood clots
in his white matter, which the doctor explains

is the network that connects grey matter to grey
matter, like cables that transmit information
between computers. His brain is already re-linking

around the damaged areas, where the story lies.
Tonight I will stand in a field holding eclipse glasses
to my eyes, watching the black dot of Venus

glide across the sun. It will be early evening.
The sun will look marigold-orange
and unremarkable, until I remember

this is the sun I'm looking at
with the very eyes my mother promised
would burst into flames if I looked right at it.

Janus

With two minutes and a Phillips head
I could unscrew that tiny strip of oak

that covers the seam in the hardwood,
the lowest of thresholds, a minor seam

in the long walkway of the hall, and yet
it is the most unnerving spot for my father

to cross, his halting gait freezing up
every time he moves from the kitchen

to the family room where he naps
in an armchair that raises and lowers

to meet him partway. No matter
where he walks now he does so with

a caregiver guiding him as he staggers
at an improbable angle, his feet shuffling

or tapping at the floor, his arms flapping
and churning the air, this hitching jig

he labors under, jittering and jerking until
he reaches that tiny, wooden lip in the floor

which he resists each time, like a bird shocked
by a reflective pane of glass. What might

he see there, caught, mute and trembling,
at the edge of something no one else can see?

Arrhythmia

It might add up to loss in the end:
a hitch in the heart, a regular hitch
in the heart. It's hard to remember
which story is which, where you left off
last time. When the next one
starts. You're hardly on the phone
anymore, lifting the receiver to greet me,
then handing it off within the minute.
Would you like to talk to your mother?
and you hardly pause for an answer,
you hardly wait a beat. It may add up
to loss in the end, a heart skipping beats.
What did I tell you before? And neither of us
can remember. Where you left off.

Deathwish

What is it like to die, my young son asks
at the dinner table, in the car,
at the grocery store, while tying his shoes,
or fiddling with the toothpaste tube. *I want
to die*, he says, and I know he doesn't mean
he wants to stop living, or he bears
unhappinesses too great to make the struggle
worth the effort. He wants to know what dying
is all about, what it feels like, and what's
on the other side, as if death were a low
fieldstone wall to clamber over. *What is it like
to die?* he asks, as if this were the first time
he'd thought of this all week, and no matter
how often he asks or I take a different tack
in my response, I'm pretending my heart
isn't pierced each time he wonders aloud
about a world I know for sure will continue on
without him. It's my death I try to prepare him for
each time I teach him one new way to live
without me: this way to fold a shirt, this way
to walk to school, this way to press the toothpaste
onto the brush. He stands on the stool
to gaze into the mirror as he brushes,
a thick, blue foam gathering at his lips.

Well

Today I waved when I drove past
even though she's too far from the road
and underground, but it seemed
the neighborly thing to do. No matter
what I believe about the afterlife
I hope she's comfortable, enjoying
her lot beside the lake, in full sun
and near enough to the service road
that my father, when I bring him
and my mother for a visit, doesn't have
too far to walk with his new cane.
Well, Joanie, he says after a long pause,
speaking to the ground, and we all
stand around, shifting our weight
and noticing the bees, the heat,
the netting over the raw dirt. Her plot
is still unmarked, but that's her grandson
there beside her, killed in a car accident
at twenty-three. Well, here are some
white and purple crocuses. Well, she was
very kind, and baked beautiful bread.
Well, it's time to go. We shuffle
across the trimmed grass to the car.
The road shimmers. The water
we think we see, midair, is just a mirage.

Syncopation

Are your parents
    home? my father
whispers. I switch

    the phone
to my other
    ear. *No, are yours?*

Bloom

What's not to love
about the crab apple tree

one day pink-budded,
the next white-bloomed,

and now its petals skittering
over the porch, the steps,

and everything? I meant
last summer to cut back

its two broken branches
after the hackberry tree

collapsed in the dark
in the rain, creaking, groaning,

then thudding heavily
on the ground with an ungodly

sound. It grazed the house,
crushing only a railing and bending

two branches of the apple tree
past mending, but by the time

I stood there with the loppers
the crab apple was winter bare,

its dead freight hidden
in so much grey matter.

Ways to Travel

Do you have the boarding passes? your father
asks, his eyes flashing. Don't argue.
Pat your jacket pocket and explain

you've got them right here, everything's
all set, and then ask him to take
another bite of his apple slice

which right now he is rubbing
against the plate the way a man
might rub a poker chip against the felt.

Except this isn't Vegas, and your father
isn't much of a gambler; even now
his mind casts about for ways

to make his world a little steadier—
packing imaginary bags, arranging
for transportation, deflecting risk. *Do you*

have the boarding passes? he'll ask again,
ready to rebuke you for your inattention
to the checklist which he runs through

endlessly. His borders have been drawing in
for years; the furthest he now travels
is to the doctor; mostly he gets wheeled

down to the pond each day to visit
with the duck, and see the willow,
and nod to joggers. In another day

you'll be gone again, walking toward the gate
with the bag you've learned to keep at hand.
He might forget you until you call,

or he might call you by another name,
or might ask aloud if you've ever written out
a check before, wondering when the two of you

might go over some banking. He wants
to make sure you can manage all
the gateways of the world. *Yes, Dad,*

I've got the tickets right here, you repeat,
tucking his napkin into his shirt against
his narrow collarbone where the pulse sits.

Hippocampus

My restless curiosity nettles the dark.
I click on the lamp, hunt for pictures
of the human brain, its folds and trajectories.
Look: the work of spatial relationships
and transferring memory to long-term storage
resides in a part of the brain named
for the seahorse, which it was thought to resemble.
And here's the amygdala, named
for an almond; that triggers fear. I twist
in the sheets and think about all the ways
my children might suffer. They are heavily asleep,
their limbs pale and askew as if
their bodies had been dropped there
from a height I'm too afraid to name.

Catch

There will be a night when I'm leaning against the doorjamb,
the dishes cleared, the good spoons returned

to the cabinet with the three hand-painted espresso cups
from pre-war Germany—a gift from a beloved great-aunt—

and a row of eleven cut-crystal wine glasses my father
carried home from a business trip to Prague.

Now that same man can hardly stand, much less
transport glasses in a carry-on without chipping a single one.

His limbs quaver even with the pills. Half-slumped in his chair,
his arm will start up again as if he were cranking the wheel

of an invisible, droning hurdy-gurdy: stabbing his mug
with a fork or shredding the newspaper. My mother

will scold him as if he should know better and hand him
a squishy ball to busy the engine of his hand. Just like that

he'll lob the ball at me which I will barely catch in time,
so stunned to see his muscles fire in the expected order.

Toss, catch, toss, catch; a dozen times we will hardly
miss a beat, the ball landing squarely in his one good hand.

My Father Used to Read Books

in two languages. My father used
to go to the gym, play handball,
do squats and push-ups with his children
on his back. My father used to play
Woody Guthrie tunes on a nylon-string guitar;
he used to play baseball with his grandchildren.
My father used to work in his lab,
pick his feet up, neaten his hair
with a small, black comb.
He used to shave his jawline.
My father used to swallow. He used
to mow the lawn, shine his shoes,
walk to work, balance the checkbook.
He used to rub his back against
doorframes, especially the one in the kitchen.
He used to whistle, shovel the walk,
carry his wallet in his back pocket.
My father used to build wooden airplanes
with his friend next door. My father used
to travel on a plane. My father used
to have a sister. Her name was Joan.
She used to remember him. She used
to laugh over the phone every time he called.

Jellyfish

O undulant, little
shockwave, rippling

moon crater, pale
as the moon, your

wave modulates
behind the glass.

This is how a mind
works: surge,

pause, dart
through the inky

current, in
motion all

the moments
we're alive.

My Father's Knees

All summer we pushed his wheelchair to the pond
so he could sit in the sun-dappled air. A wide brim shaded

his face, sunglasses cut the glare, but his knees
tanned to a brown as burnished as the walnut cabinet

he built one summer, sawdust sheeting the patio
where he'd set up the bandsaw, waking my sister

from her nap with its high whine. We weren't allowed
to touch the record player, but years later,

after I'd watched him a thousand times, and the house
was empty, I lifted the arm as steadily as

I could above the spinning record, aiming
the needle into the narrow, silent space.

Blue

Twice a year we come visiting, flying out of the blue
into the green of Virginia, where you are dying out of the blue.

Some days you know us; some days you don't. *Good morning!*
I begin the day. *I miss my mom*, you say, sighing, out of the blue.

I miss my dad, I answer, grinning, then prattle about the weather,
last night's Cubs game, local traffic, my chatter multiplying out of the blue.

You've fallen more times than I can count: against the counter,
out of the chair, against the radiator, crying out of the blue.

Evening is harder. You're stiff in your chair, one arm pistoning,
jaws working in the air, your tremors amplifying out of the blue.

Your grip on your spoon is strong, though your arm shakes.
You hardly blink anymore, eyeing out of the blue.

My mother asks if she should ask for a prognosis,
by which she means time left. *No*, I say, lying out of the blue.

You've been clutching the newspaper all morning, scanning
the headlines. Words are mystifying out of the blue.

Your fingertips stroke my cheek; *Ann,* you say,
perhaps by accident, but getting it right out of the blue.

The Pond

Maybe a fox. Or maybe a hawk
snatched the duck from her nest.
The drake broods on the gray water.
On the far bank a fisherman
stands in the shadows, his line
glinting. My father, in his wildness,
likes to sit by the water and tap his feet
against the footplates of his wheelchair.
Today he explains that once, walking
to kindergarten, he watched a cop shoot
a barking dog. It may have been rabid.
The dog dropped to the ground.
Even then my father understood
there was no way of turning back.

Signals and Feedback

Why I've been poring over your articles all evening
escapes me. I'm annoyed I can't find anything
to understand. I can't get behind the paywalls
of most journals, or make head or tails of abstracts.
I still don't get what it was you spent your life
discovering. There was a night two years ago,
you hovered in the kitchen while we tidied up
after dinner guests, and you described why
prime numbers are not chaotic, how
to know whether the dynamics of a system
are regular or not, and how long it takes to lose
the ability to predict future behavior.
I knew it then: this was a last conversation
of its kind. I followed you as long as I could.

Afterlife

Whose music will he hear once
he is dead, and we are rowing him
or whatever remains of him,

the him-not-him, to meet whatever
is there? What will be there to greet him?
Nothing, my husband says. *God*,

my friend says. *Heaven*, my son says,
though I don't know what he means
by heaven and I'd love a glossy brochure

like those my father would let me
pick out one of at the rest stops.
In the backseat I'd trace the blue

on the map, following our sweltering course
from the worn blue mountains of Virginia
through the industrial wasteland of Charleston,

the junctions of Indianapolis, up through
the prairies of Illinois. All the windows
stayed rolled down so when we finally

pulled off toward the motel, that roaring
was still all we heard, and for a while
it was so hard to talk no one did, even though

we had questions and we knew Dad
could explain: *How is glass made?*
Who built the road through the mountain?

Why are there water towers? The roaring
buffeted our ears as we tried to sleep.
That music. Whose music is that?

Blue Again

Today I'm angry over this slow loss of you.
Your body, gray and gaunter. There's less of you.

You gaze at the sports pages every morning
but don't read a word; letters are chaos to you.

Friends bring salmon, potatoes, green beans.
Most land in your aproned lap, making a mess of you.

I thumb through your songbooks, sing the tunes
I can still pick out, fumbling through notes and rests of you.

Each goodbye is harder now.
I don't know when I'll see the last of you.

You squint at me across the table. *Ann*, I prompt.
My mouth, your mouth. A palimpsest of you.

Red Geraniums

My children have been excused from the table,
have picked up their plates, half-nudging their chairs in
with their narrow hips, and jangled their silverware
all the way to the sink. My mother is already
in the sideyard picking through the ivy, a pair
of yellow scissors in one hand. She leans over to check
the pots of geraniums, stroking the lobes
of their dark green leaves. I'm sitting
by my father's wheelchair holding out a spoon.
His dinner bowl is still half full. He's been chewing
a long time and won't open his mouth
for more. His left wrist crimps against his ribcage,
and he lists in his chair as he works his jaws.
Let's stop all this nonsense, he blurts out hoarsely,
his slate blue eyes swiveling to meet mine,
and whether he means our slow progress
through this meal or more, I can't say. There's rice
in his beard and in his lap. I kneel and tell him
if he needs to rest he should rest, and if he's ready
he should let go, that I love him and wish him peace.
The spoon dangles between us. Two squirrels
bicker in the holly tree outside the open window.
My father widens his eyes a fraction and stares at me,
hardly blinking, and I will myself not to look away,
hoping like hell at least one of us has understood.

Torso of a Male Athlete (The Oil Pourer)

Marble, Roman, 1st–2nd century AD
after Athens, Greece, late 4th-century BC original

My son stares a moment at the marble statue
behind the glass, then nudges me and whispers,
Who'd want to make a naked guy, I mean, his parts...
marveling at how infinitely weird adults are.
In fact, the man's *parts* have broken off, as have
his head, his arms, his entire left leg, and his right leg
below the knee. Even his nipples have worn
away. It's amazing there's enough to respond to:
a sculpted chest, abdomen, the grooves
where his thighs connect to where his penis
and scrotum hung. Most of my father's limbs
are frozen as if stone, his stiff legs crooked
but not bending, his left arm kinked against his side
with his hand bent double against his chest.
We tuck pillows where we can, turning him
from side to side to help the bedsores heal
but they keep breaking in. We brush his teeth.
We slide a washcloth over his face, his armpits,
his groin, then dab lotion on his untorn skin.
This athlete, the museum placard tells me,
stands in a moment of calm, anointing himself
before a competition. His missing hands burnish
his chest with oil. Even through the glass
I sense his equilibrium, a tautness that persuades me
he's present in this body, still poised and alert.

My Father's Hair

He taught us to never touch
his hair: combed and set
with a touch of spray
he wouldn't discuss using.
But once illness took away
his vanity, not to mention
his ability to hold a comb,
Mom bought clippers.
His eyes were wide beneath
his soft, white fringe. We ran
our fingers through it when
we sat with him and there
was nothing else to say.

Last Day

His teeth are slicked with white glaze.
I scrape them with the tip of a tiny red sponge

on a stick. Keeping the body
clean is not the same as comfortable,

but what else is there to do? The radio's
low adagios, a soft lamp. Someone

raises the blinds. We change the sheets,
rolling him carefully from one side to the other.

I hold his face to keep it from pressing
against the bedrails, then drag some Vaseline

across his cracked lips. His dark breath
shirrs the pillowcase. Yesterday he whispered

Will there be trees there? and my sister
said yes, and held his hand. In retrospect

it was so obvious when he edged his bent legs
off the bed he meant to head outside. Maybe

we should have wheeled his bed into the grass;
instead we tucked the sheets gently in around him.

The broad leaves of the catalpa
fanned in the heat. I stood at his window

and saw the inroads the caterpillars had made,
gnawing the leaves on an entire limb

down to bare spines. Maybe he saw waving green.
Maybe he just remembered the green was there.

Afterward

Was it midnight when I clicked on
the baby monitor? The video flickered on,

volume dialed down to zero, and there
in grainy black and white was my mother

bent over my father's bed again, stroking
the crook of his left elbow where the heat

from his body pooled. The hospice nurse
had sat with us an hour, then helped change him

into his finishing clothes. I'd lifted his legs
which were lighter than they'd been

in all the times I'd helped to lift them.
I'd carefully slid the white, pinstriped cotton

over his feet where the skin was breaking,
fabric too sheer to be mended.

The Undertakers

Ushering the two hastily-suited men
over the threshold of the quiet house,

I showed them to my father's room
where my sister waited, then returned

to the kitchen where my mother was leaning
her forearms on the honey-wooden table,

her forehead propped up by her thumbs.
She stared at nothing. I heard the men

moving in the adjacent room, fumbling,
their voices low, heard the squeal

of one wayward wheel on the black gurney
which made me think of shopping carts,

how one errant wheel can make a tiny,
effective madness of an errand.

My mother stared at nothing,
made a roof over nothing with the arch

of her head and shoulders over the table.
The two men shuffled and grunted,

the gurney squeaked, and they wheeled
my father out of the house, a dark blue blanket

cuffed beneath his chin as if to keep
his last warmth with him. I wished

I'd been there in that room to see them hoist
and fumble with this thing that was

and wasn't him, to see the work of it,
to see the weight—what weight

he had there in the end—register with these
two men who'd dressed hurriedly

in the dark of their own houses,
then driven to ours to collect our dead.

I held the screen door open as they slid
him into the further darkness, where

the gray tree frogs trilled and echoed,
invisible in the tree-stitched yard.

Aftermath

From Old English: *a second crop*
of grass grown after an earlier
crop in the same season has been harvested.
The house ticks, dishwasher
thrumming, kitchen dark. A window
rattles, loose in its casing. We've
retreated to our separate rooms.
To ask who built the machinery
of the world implies a system.
The system changes over time.
After the mowing, something returns:
grasses, meadow, anthill, hive.

Notes

The Folk Songs of North America (1960) is a 623-page anthology of American folk songs compiled by ethnomusicologist Alan Lomax. He and his father, John Lomax, collected recordings of folk and blues musicians around the US, championing music and musicians that fell outside the dominant paradigm. Their field recordings, oral histories, interviews, and other documents are archived at the Library of Congress. Alan Lomax was also a consultant for Carl Sagan's Golden Record project, which sent into space a sampling of music from around the world.

Torso of a Male Athlete (The Oil Pourer) is a marble sculpture at the Milwaukee Art Museum, Milwaukee, WI.

Acknowledgments

Versions of these poems have appeared in the following journals, occasionally under different titles. Many thanks to the editors for their kind attention.

Beloit Poetry Journal: "My Father Used to Read Books"

Box Journal: "Torso of a Male Athlete (The Oil Pourer)"

The Briar Cliff Review: "Bloom"

HOOT: "I Still Address You Even Though I'm Talking To Myself"

Ilanot Review: "Green"

Mom Egg Review: "Time and Temperature"

Northwest Review: "June 19"

Pacifica Literary Review: "Someone To Watch Over Me"

Raleigh Review: "Ways to Travel"

River Styx: "My Father's Hair"

Rogue Agent: "Hippocampus"

Salamander: "Red Geranium," *The Folk Songs of North America*"

Spoon River Poetry Review: "Afterlife," "Janus," "Blue," "Rust," "The Pond," "Last Day"

The Night Heron Barks: "Wind Farms"

Third Wednesday: "Azalea, Dogwood, Maple, Boxwood," "How to Get There," "Second Grade," "The Lessons"

West Branch: "My Father's Knees," "Transit of Venus"

"Potential Energy" appears on the Facebook page *My Cubs Story*.

Thank you also to the many people who helped guide and support me and this book to this moment:

> my father, John "Jack" Hudson, whose strength and steadfastness supports me still;
>
> my mother, Janette Hudson, who tended to my father with fierce love and attention, and allowed him to live and die with dignity and peace at home as he wished;
>
> my amazing sisters, Barbara and Sarah Hudson, who have their own stories to tell about this time and have generously given me space to tell mine;
>
> my father's doctors, nurses, caregivers, colleagues, and friends, who supported him through his illness and helped his life stay rich and meaningful;
>
> the Michael J. Fox Foundation, a transformative organization dedicated to finding treatment and ultimately a cure for Parkinson's;
>
> the Virginia Center for the Creative Arts, for the generous gift of time and space to revise many of these poems and find a shape for the manuscript, and to the many brilliant writers and artists there who inspired and challenged me;
>
> my Next Page Press family for being such a welcoming, talented collective, and especially Laura Van Prooyen, whose keen eye and open heart have made this book so much stronger and focused;
>
> my *Rhino* crash, for working so carefully and caringly to lift amazing poems up to the world;
>
> my family of poets, many of whom have so generously given their time, attention, and expertise to these poems: Liz Ahl, Joanne Diaz, Tara Ebrahimi, Jan Freeman, Lindsay Garbutt, Willie James, Matthew Kelsey, Cate Lycurgus, Faisal Mohyuddin, Jacob Saenz, Jeremy Schmidt, Noah Stetzer, Casey Thayer, and Laura Van Prooyen. I miss you, Jeff Oaks;
>
> and to Allen, Rae, and Joshua, who have added and added immeasurably to my world.

About the Author

Ann Hudson is the author of *The Armillary Sphere* (Ohio UP) and *Glow* (Next Page Press). Her poems have appeared in *Beloit Poetry Journal*, *Orion*, *Crab Orchard Review*, *Colorado Review*, *North American Review*, *Prairie Schooner*, *Shenandoah*, *SWWIM*, *Tinderbox*, *West Branch*, and elsewhere. She is a teaching artist with Hive Center for the Book Arts in Evanston, IL, and a senior editor for *Rhino*.

www.ingramcontent.com/pod-product-compliance
Lightning Source LLC
Chambersburg PA
CBHW030317100526
44585CB00014BA/955